Velvet Concord

Velvet
The Little French

Velvet's Concept drawn from the book
Izvy: A Rock Star by Dyva Gibbs

Illustrations by The Little French

Copyright Little French's Media LLC 2024

Velvet Concord was a
unique blend of rap & pop

elvet Concord

Secret passions and daring truths

Velvet Concord

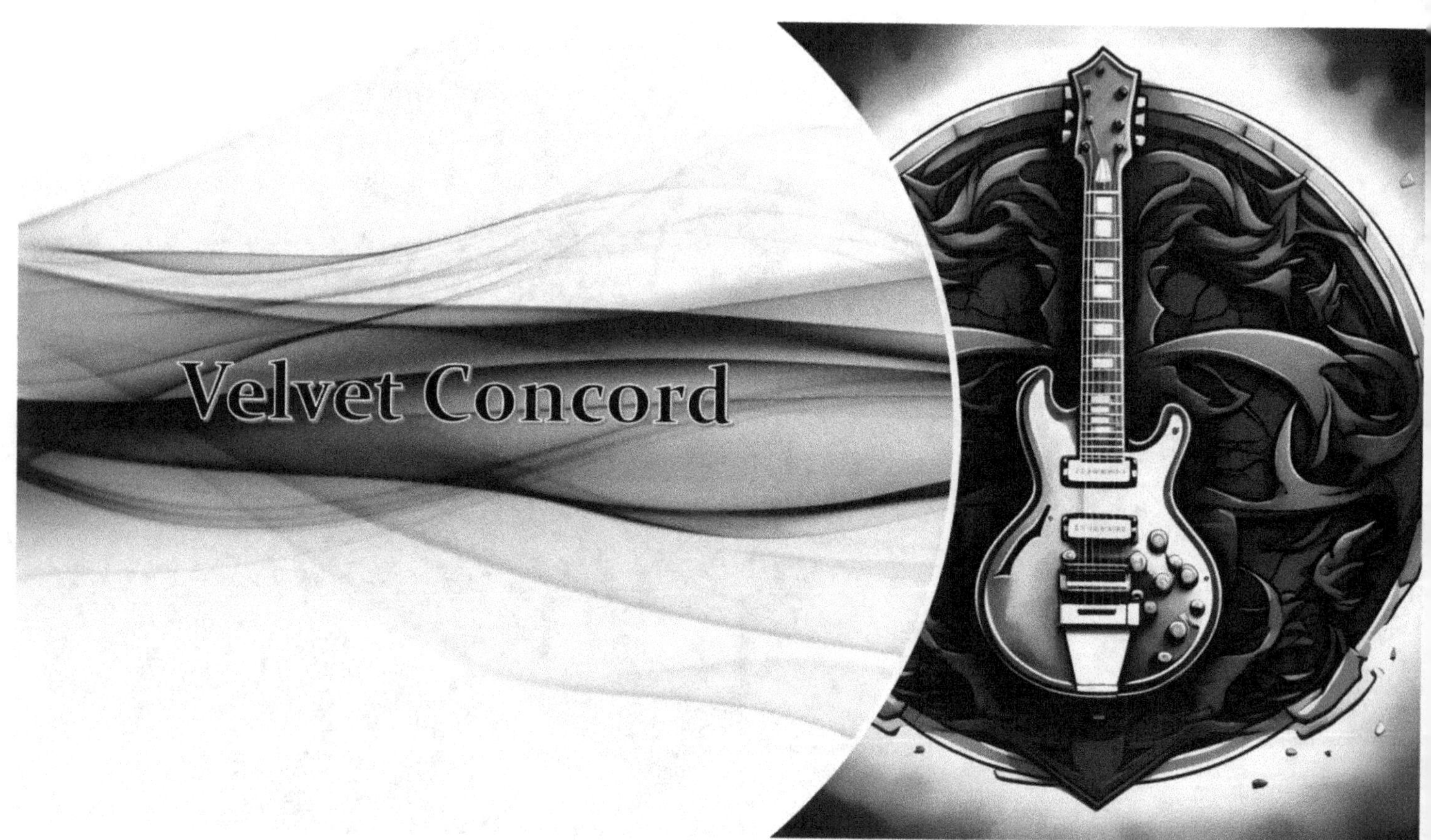

21 Records

Velvet Concord

New York Hot Tracks

Velvet Concord

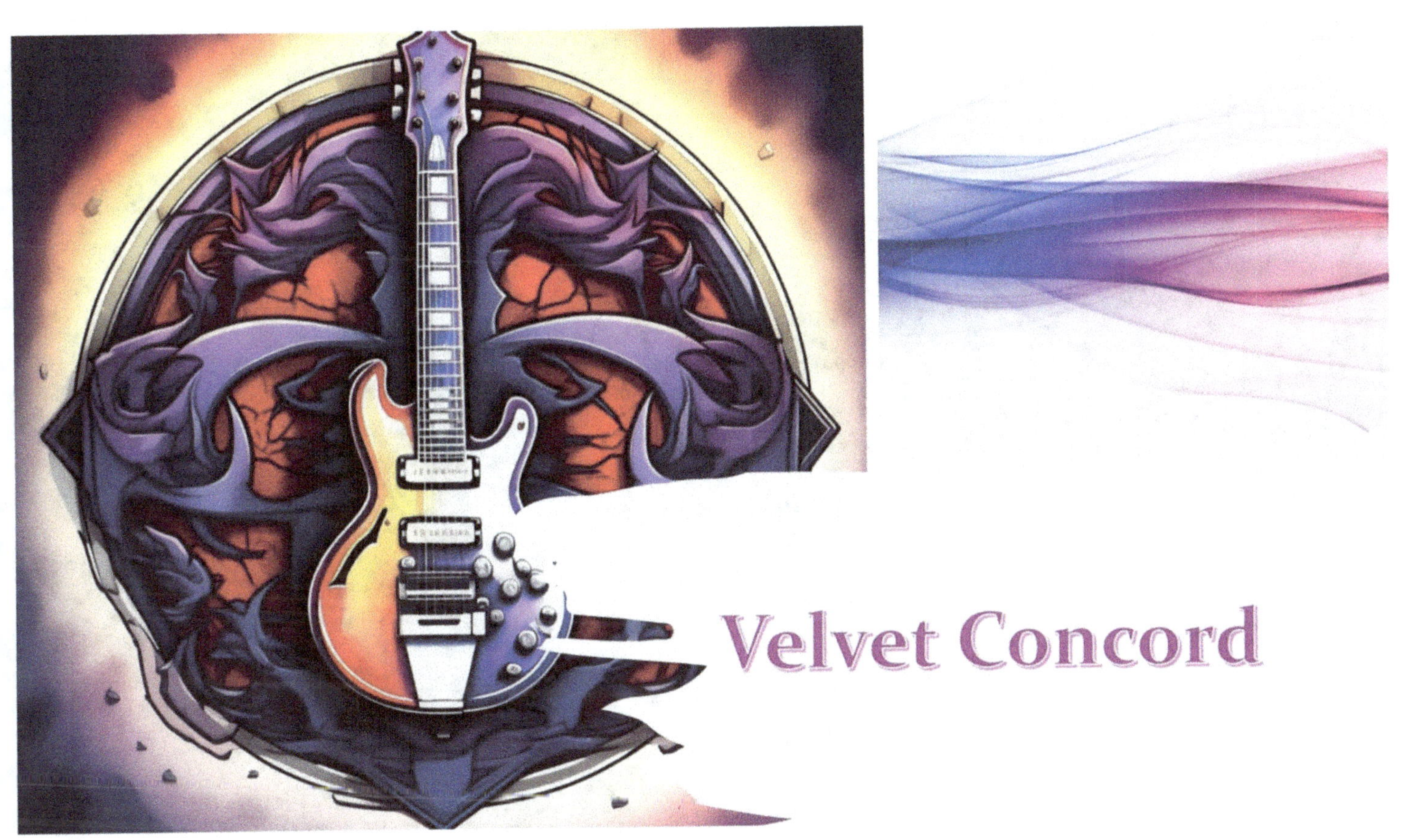

Velvet Concord

Velvet Concord

Music is a powerful force
that can bring people together

Velvet Concord

Between You & Me

Velvet Concord

Age and experience do not
have to dim the creative spark

Velvet Concord

Failure can lead to success

Velvet Concord

VTD EIIIEEI

Velvet

Velvet Concord

Easy to consume and leaves you
feeling empty inside

Velvet Concord

Songs were catchy, danceable, and had a positive message

Velvet Concord

I'm gonna let myself go

Velvet

I can't get enough

Velvet

I'm the one who makes
you lose control

Velvet

He was a shield against
the world's attack

Velvet

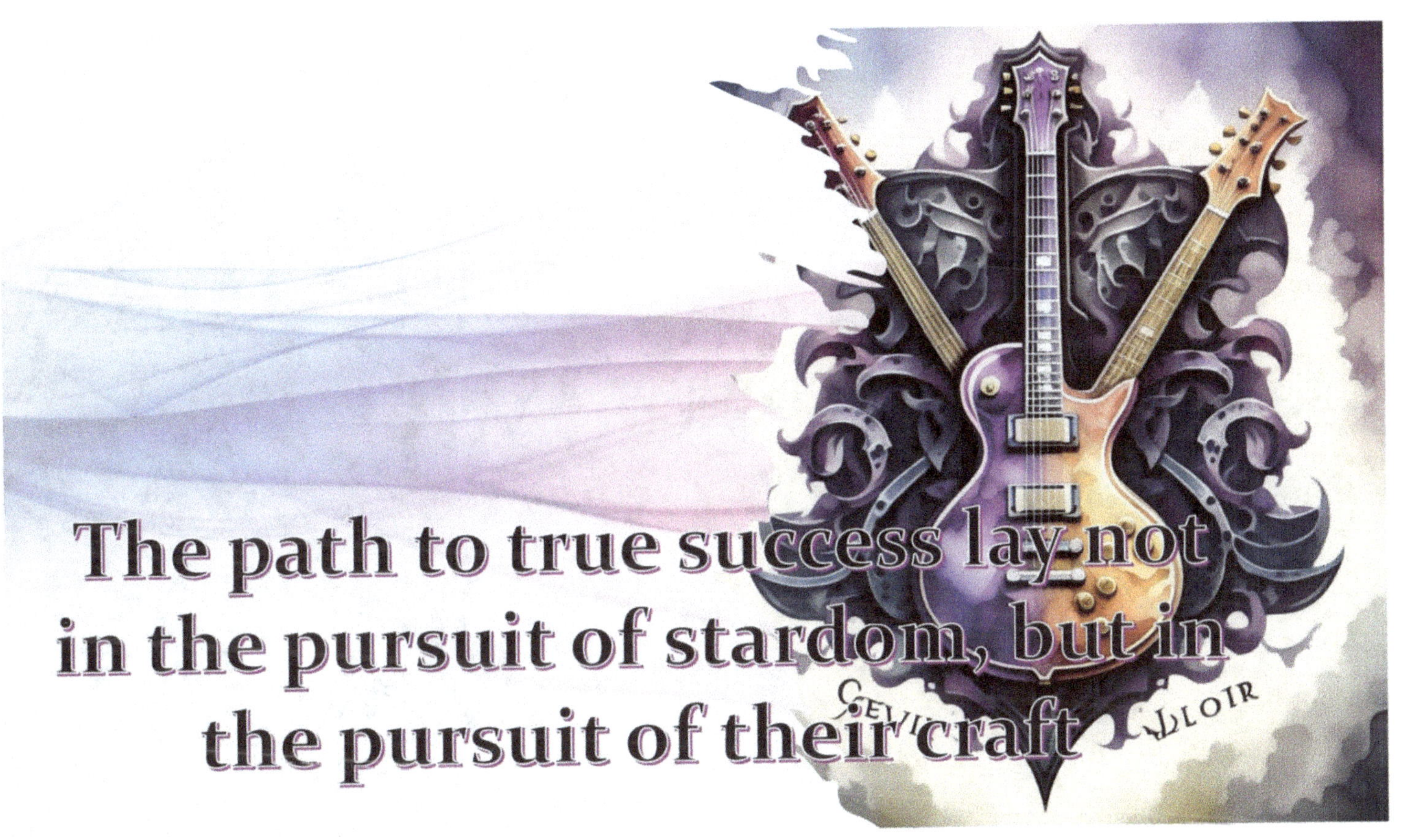

The path to true success lay not in the pursuit of stardom, but in the pursuit of their craft

Velvet Concord

Silent departure

Velvet Concord

Izvi's success:
a bitter pill to swallow

Velvet Concord

Her nails dug into his back

Velvet Concord

After a wild night out

Velvet Concord

Mia- the chorus girl
bombarded with paparazzi
and hounded by reporters

Velvet Concord

The princess wasn't
in a fairytale gown
as he imagined

Velvet Concord

VOCCCOCODR
Velvet

Velvet

A charity event

Velvet

Mia's music had the
power to touch lives

Velvet

He realized that his sexual
orientation was not a choice

Velvet

The end of the beginning

Velvet

Emotion of loss & disillusionment

Velvet

The End

Velvet

His music transcended
the boundaries of genre

Velvet Concord

Her music spoke to
the hearts of others

Velvet Concord

Liam's debut solo album
is a nostalgic echo of
his former band

Velvet Concord

A transformative experience, shaping their perspectives on life and love

Velvet Concord

The fallout from a
scandal brought about
a wave of backlash

Velvet

The princess' acceptance and support empowered him to face his challanges

Velvet

Mia is the ultimate pop chameleon

Velvet Concord

Liam's music is a frustrating
case of wasted potential

Velvet Concord

Master of My Destiny
was a departure from
his earlier pop work

Velvet Concord

Music was once a source
of joy and expression

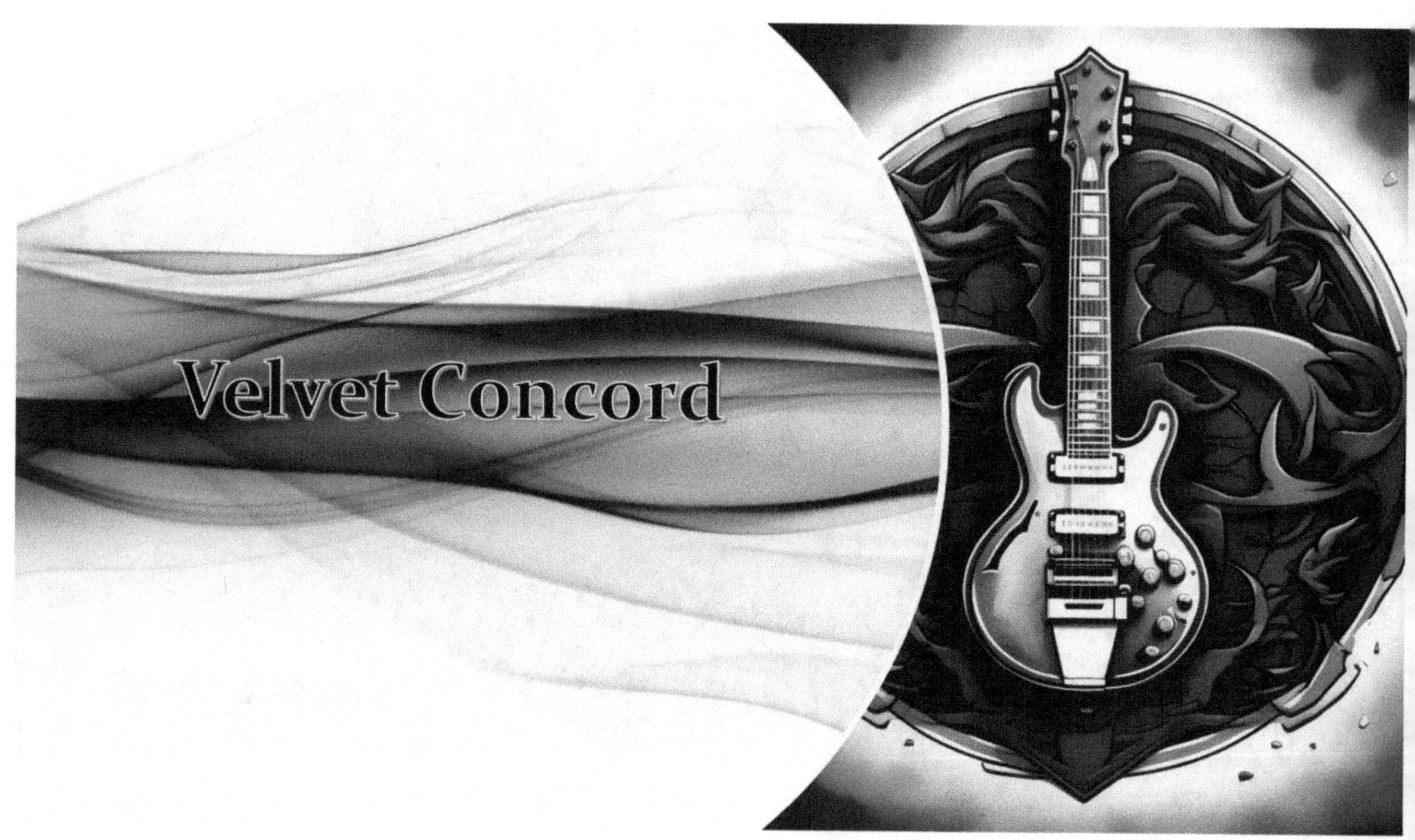

Velvet Concord

He was a single thread woven into the vast fabric of human experience

Velvet

The Past

Velvet

Don't let it get you down
Don't give up

Velvet

The world is changing fast
It's hard to keep up

Velvet

Go with the changes

Velvet

We can play our music

Velvet Concord

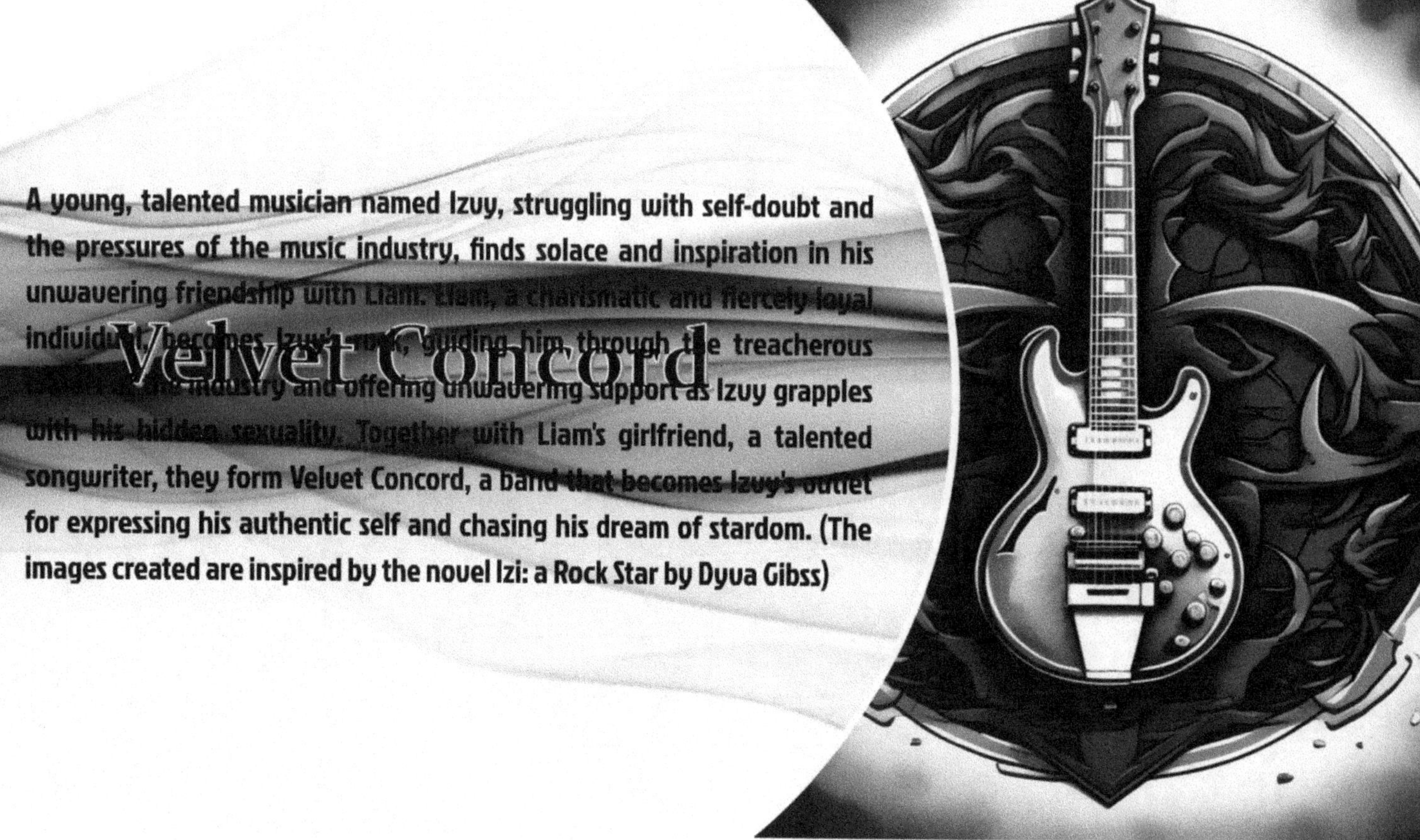

A young, talented musician named Izuy, struggling with self-doubt and the pressures of the music industry, finds solace and inspiration in his unwavering friendship with Liam. Liam, a charismatic and fiercely loyal individual, becomes Izuy's rock, guiding him through the treacherous waters of the industry and offering unwavering support as Izuy grapples with his hidden sexuality. Together with Liam's girlfriend, a talented songwriter, they form Velvet Concord, a band that becomes Izuy's outlet for expressing his authentic self and chasing his dream of stardom. (The images created are inspired by the novel Izi: a Rock Star by Dyva Gibss)